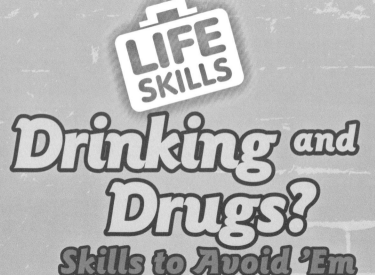

LIFE SKILLS

Drinking and Drugs?
Skills to Avoid 'Em and Stay Cool

Louise Spilsbury

Enslow Publishing

101 W. 23rd Street
Suite 240
New York, NY 10011
USA

enslow.com

Published in 2019 by Enslow Publishing, LLC.
101 W. 23rd Street, Suite 240, New York, NY 10011

Cataloging-in-Publication Data

Names: Spilsbury, Louise.
Title: Drinking and drugs? skills to avoid 'em and stay cool / Louise Spilsbury.
Description: New York : Enslow Publishing, 2019. | Series: Life skills | Includes index.
Identifiers: ISBN 9780766099722 (pbk.) | ISBN 9780766099715 (library bound)
Subjects: LCSH: Drugs--Juvenile literature. | Alcohol--Juvenile literature.
Classification: LCC RM301.S65 2019 | DDC 363.45--dc23

Printed in the United States of America

To Our Readers: We have done our best to make sure all website addresses in this book were active and appropriate when we went to press. However, the author and the publisher have no control over and assume no liability for the material available on those websites or on any websites they may link to. Any comments or suggestions can be sent by e-mail to customerservice@enslow.com.

Photo Credits: Cover: Shutterstock: Creativa Images; Inside: Shutterstock: Antoniodiaz 8, A Yakovlev 41, Berczy04 14t, Christian Bertrand 30, Bikeriderlondon 45, Billion Photos 4, Diego Cervo 33, Cliparea/Custom Media 17, Dani3315 5, Forbis 15, Sergey Goruppa 24, Hanzi-mor 12, Iordani 1, 26, Ben Jeayes 44, Sebastian Kaulitzki 25, Piotr Krzeslak 16, Littleny 22, MarinaP 18, Michaeljung 28, Monkey Business Images 38, Monstar Studio 31, Naeblys 23, Nehopelon 40, Nerthuz 19, Nevodka 10, Photographee.eu 21, 27, 34, 43, Photopixel 14b, Phovoir 37, Prill 13, Rawpixel.com 6, 36, Romaset 9, Sabphoto 29, SpeedKingz 32, Stockelements 20, Syda Productions 11, 39, Chepko Danil Vitalevich 42, Voyagerix 7, Vladimir Wrangel 35.

Contents

Chapter 1
What Are Drugs?

A drug is any **chemical** that affects the way your body works. A drug starts to work after it has passed into your blood, and from there into your brain. When drugs are inside the brain, they can affect the messages that the brain **cells** send to each other, and to the rest of the body. There are thousands of different kinds of drugs, and they affect the body in different ways. Some of these drugs can help the body, but others can harm it.

LEGAL AND ILLEGAL DRUGS

Most of the drugs that scientists have developed over the years have mainly good effects, such as the aspirin people can take to cure a headache. Nonetheless, even the **legal** drugs can have bad effects if taken incorrectly. The alcohol in wine and beer, the caffeine in tea and coffee, and the nicotine in cigarettes are all drugs that are legal but that can have negative effects. Some drugs, such as cocaine, have such a serious and dangerous effect on the body that they are **illegal**. When you hear someone talking about a "drug problem," they are usually referring to people using illegal drugs like this. Illegal drugs are not good for adults, but they are especially bad for young people, because their bodies are still growing.

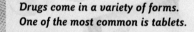

Drugs come in a variety of forms. One of the most common is tablets.

NATURAL DRUGS

Some drugs can be extracted from natural sources, and they have been used by humans for a long time. In Peru and the Andes, millions of people chew coca leaves and drink coca tea without problems. The coca leaf in its natural form is a harmless and mild **stimulant** that suppresses hunger, thirst, pain, and tiredness. But the illegal drug known as cocaine that can be extracted from the coca leaf is a very dangerous drug, and it kills many people around the world.

Peoples in the Andean region have chewed the coca leaf for centuries. Today, the United States wants Peru to stop growing coca and to switch to other crops, because coca can be used to make the illegal drug cocaine. However, coca itself is not a drug, and many farmers rely on it to survive.

Social Drugs

Social drugs are ones that people use or take in social situations. People often take these drugs to help them relax, or to make them feel they have more energy. The two main social drugs are caffeine-based drinks and nicotine. Nicotine and caffeine are both stimulants, drugs that increase brain activity and make people feel more alert.

CAFFEINE KICKS

Caffeine is found in coffee, tea, chocolate, some sodas, and "energy" drinks. Caffeine works by blocking the chemical signals in the brain that make people feel sleepy, so it makes them feel more alert. An adult drinking four or five cups of tea or coffee each day should have no bad **side effects** from caffeine, but caffeine is **addictive**, and people can suffer from headaches, tiredness, and loss of concentration when they do not have it. Drinking too much caffeine can make adults anxious and shaky, cause increased heartbeat and **blood pressure**, and give them an upset stomach. Caffeine is also a **diuretic**, meaning it makes people urinate more. This can cause **dehydration**, when the body does not work properly because it does not have enough water. Caffeine may be safe for most adults in small amounts, but it is definitely not good for children.

Drinking up to five cups of caffeinated beverages daily such as tea and coffee should do an adult no harm, though it can be addictive.

Cigarettes contain nicotine as well as about 4,000 other chemicals, many of which are harmful to the body.

CIGARETTES AND NICOTINE

When a person **inhales** tobacco smoke from a cigarette, the nicotine travels via the **lungs** to the brain in about seven seconds. Nicotine works like a naturally-occurring brain chemical, and gives smokers a brief feeling of pleasure. The problem is that smoking kills. Tobacco smoke contains many substances that cause **cancer**. Smoking increases the risk of lung cancer, mouth cancer, and throat cancer, and also of heart and lung disease. Tobacco cigarettes are the leading cause of preventable deaths in the United States. Nicotine is highly addictive, and once you start smoking, it is hard to stop. So say no to cigarettes from the start!

Medicinal Drugs

Medicinal drugs are drugs used to relieve disease and illness, and they are carefully and extensively tested before they are given to patients. Medicines are legal drugs that doctors can **prescribe** for a patient, or that people can buy over the counter at a pharmacy or even in a store. Although these drugs are legal, it is against the law to buy them from people who are selling them illegally, or to misuse them and take them for anything other than medical reasons. Taking any medicine in a way not recommended by a doctor can be dangerous.

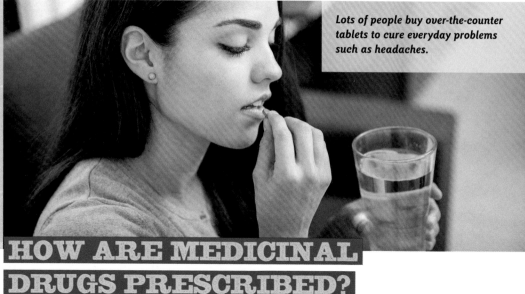

Lots of people buy over-the-counter tablets to cure everyday problems such as headaches.

HOW ARE MEDICINAL DRUGS PRESCRIBED?

Only the people who have been prescribed medicinal drugs by a doctor should take them. Those drugs are only safe for the people who have prescriptions for them. Before prescribing the medicine, a doctor has **examined** the patient and determined which sort of medicine to give them, and the correct dose required for their medical condition. The doctor has also taken into account other factors specific to that particular patient, such as their weight and lifestyle, before prescribing it. They warn the patient to avoid certain things while on the medicine, such as drinking alcohol, smoking, or taking other medications, and they monitor the patient in case they suffer side effects that could be dangerous. Taking medicine not prescribed for you is illegal and can be very dangerous. It can even kill you.

Skills for Life

- **Read the labels!** Over-the-counter medications can be dangerous, too. Taking the recommended dose for your age, weight, and health problem should be fine, but taking any more can cause health problems.
- **Listen to your doctor!** Take the full course of prescribed drugs as directed by the doctor or pharmacist, even if you feel better, unless a doctor tells you otherwise. If you stop taking an **antibiotic** partway through a treatment, the **bacteria** can become **resistant** to the antibiotic.

Doctors check a patient's general health carefully so they can be sure to prescribe the correct medicine for them.

Chapter 2
Different Drugs

There are many different kinds of drugs, and people use or take them in different ways. Most people who have a "drug problem" use illegal drugs such as cocaine, LSD, crystal meth, or heroin. In some states in the US, adults can legally use marijuana if a doctor has recommended it for a particular illness. In others, adults can legally use marijuana recreationally. In some states, marijuana is illegal for medical or recreational use.

WHAT IS MARIJUANA?

Marijuana is made from the leaves, stems, seeds, and flowers of the hemp plant. It is also sometimes called cannabis, weed, grass, pot, and other names. Marijuana is smoked in a hand-rolled cigarette or in a pipe. It can be mixed into foods, or brewed as a tea. When someone smokes marijuana, a chemical called tetrahydrocannabinol (THC) travels through the lungs and blood to the brain and other body **organs**. THC affects how the brain works, and causes people to feel chilled out, happy, and relaxed. The problem is that marijuana can have some harmful effects on the mind and body, and can have long-term negative impacts.

The THC in marijuana is sometimes used to make pills that help relieve pain, sickness, muscle stiffness, or problems with movement in patients with some conditions.

Smoking marijuana can be harmful to children and teenagers.

WHAT ARE THE PROBLEMS WITH MARIJUANA?

In some cases, marijuana can make people feel very anxious, make it harder to concentrate or learn, make their memory worse, and make them feel less motivated. It can make some people **paranoid**, which means they feel like someone is out to hurt them or is plotting against them, and it can cause **hallucinations**, when people see, hear, or feel things that are not real. Marijuana raises the body's heart rate and blood pressure. Marijuana can cause serious long-term brain problems in children and teenagers, whose brains are still developing. Smoking marijuana may also be bad for the lungs. Scientists are still researching whether marijuana increases the risk of diseases such as lung cancer. In some states, possessing marijuana can also land you in jail.

Sniffing Substances

There are some drugs that people sniff, or inhale, rather than injecting or smoking them. These are known as **inhalants**. Some substances people inhale are the chemical vapors made by common household substances such as glue, nail polish remover, aerosols, gasoline, and a whole range of other cleaners and chemicals.

If you know a friend is using inhalants, tell them they need help and tell an adult. You could save their life.

WHY DO PEOPLE USE INHALANTS?

Inhalants are **depressants**. This means that they slow down the brain and body's responses. People inhale these substances because they can cause a quick feeling of being light-headed, like being drunk on alcohol, and make people feel more relaxed. These effects do not last long, at most thirty to forty-five minutes, and afterward people feel sleepy, dizzy, and confused. Unfortunately, because these household substances are lying around in millions of our kitchens and garages, people do not always understand how dangerous they can be.

Some of the inhalants people buy are flammable, so there is a real risk of burns and explosions, especially in an enclosed space or if someone nearby is smoking.

DANGER OF DEATH

The substances used as inhalants are safe when they are used for the things they were designed to do, and when they are handled properly. For example, glue is harmless when used to stick sheets of paper together. However, when they are inhaled it is an entirely different story. Then they become incredibly dangerous. Sniffing inhalants can damage the muscles, liver, kidneys, and brain, and it can even kill you. Death can happen so quickly that there is not even time to get someone to the hospital for help. Some people have even been killed after just one sniff. This is commonly known as Sudden Sniffing Death Syndrome. Inhalants can affect the heart, and they can also kill when users pass out and choke on their own vomit. People sometimes think they will be OK if they only have a little, but it is hard to control the amount taken in, and even just a little too much can put people in a **coma**, or kill them.

The Most Dangerous Drugs

There are many different dangers from drugs, and even safe or legal drugs such as medicines can be dangerous when taken in large doses, or by the wrong people. In terms of numbers of people who are killed by a drug, nicotine is the biggest killer because when people smoke tobacco over a long period, they greatly increase their risk of getting cancer. However, the most dangerous illegal drugs are considered to be heroin and a type of cocaine called crack.

COCAINE

There are several different kinds of cocaine, including crack. They are all powerful stimulants, which speed up the way the mind and body work, temporarily making people feel good. The effects wear off very quickly, leaving the user very depressed and nervous. This feeling can last for days, so people start to **crave** cocaine because they think that is the only way they will feel good again. People inhale cocaine, snort it through their nose, or inject it into a vein using a syringe. Crack is smoked in a pipe.

Cocaine looks like a fine white powder. Dealers often mix it with things like cornstarch, talcum powder, or flour to make more money.

HEROIN

Heroin is made from a chemical called morphine, which is found in the opium poppy plant. Doctors use morphine sometimes as a painkiller, to soothe patients in extreme pain. A small dose of heroin can make people feel warm and happy. More heroin makes people feel sleepy and very relaxed. Heroin is highly addictive, and people can quickly get hooked. Many people get very dizzy and sick when they first try it.

The opium used to make heroin comes from inside the pod of the opium poppy plant.

Skills for Life

Knowing about the risks of these dangerous drugs helps you to understand why you do not want to try them.

- Cocaine makes people very depressed and is highly addictive. Taking a lot of cocaine can raise the body's temperature, and cause people to have fits, a heart attack, and heart failure.
- Heroin can stop your breathing and kill you, if you take too much.

Chapter 3
All About Alcohol

Drinking alcoholic drinks such as beer, wine, and spirits is dangerous for young people. It sometimes causes health risks and other problems for adults, too. The problem is that TV shows and advertisements often show drinking as a fun, cool thing to do. Taken in moderation, adults can enjoy alcohol safely, but it is very unsafe for young people to drink it while their bodies are still growing. Doctors advise that children and young people should avoid alcohol completely until they become adults.

Even though drinking alcohol is legal and mostly safe for adults, the government still has guidelines about how much adults can drink before they start to do themselves harm.

HOW ALCOHOL CHANGES YOU

The scientific name for the alcohol in alcoholic drinks is ethanol. Ethanol is a depressant, which means it slows down signals in the **nerves** and brain and thus slows down a person's responses in all kinds of ways. Small amounts of alcohol can reduce feelings of anxiety, and help some adults to relax. It also reduces **inhibitions**, which can help people to feel more sociable around other people. The more alcohol a person drinks, the more effect it has on them.

MAKING MISTAKES AND TAKING RISKS

Alcohol reduces a person's inhibitions and changes their ability to think, speak, and see properly. After a few drinks, people may start to slur their words when they speak. They may have trouble walking properly, and lose their balance when they try to stand up. Alcohol can exaggerate our emotions, so people might become very tearful, or get into an argument. Drinking alcohol can make people lose their **self-control**, and do stupid or dangerous things. They might hurt themselves or other people. Drinking too much alcohol can also leave you at risk of being abused or hurt by others. People often have accidents while they are drunk, leading to injuries, and sometimes these accidents are **fatal**.

Getting drunk is a risky behavior, however old you are, because it reduces your ability to think and react, which can lead to mistakes.

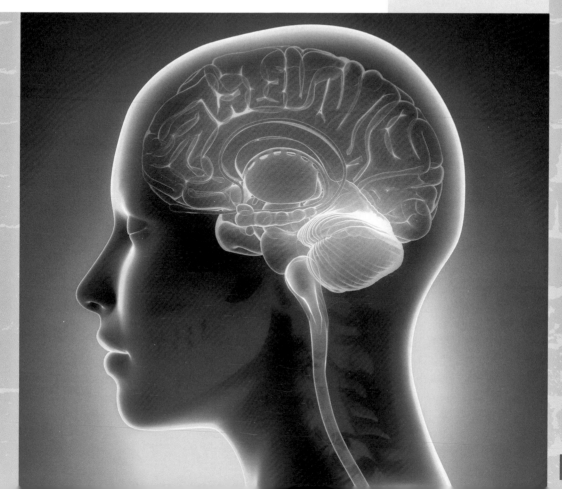

How Alcohol Affects the Body

The short-term effects of alcohol can last for a day or two, depending on how much a person drinks. Drinking can make people vomit, and they usually wake up with a **hangover**, which means they are dehydrated, feel dreadful, and cannot function properly. They may not remember what happened or what they did when they were drunk. For some people, the short-term effects of drinking are more serious, and the first time they drink alcohol is their last. Drinking too much alcohol on a single occasion can give you alcohol poisoning.

Drinking too much can cause splitting headaches, vomiting, dizziness, and dehydration.

ALCOHOL POISONING

Every time someone drinks alcohol, their liver has to filter it out of their blood. The body absorbs alcohol more quickly than food, but the body can still only process a small amount of alcohol per hour. If someone drinks a lot of alcohol over a short space of time, the body does not have time to process it all. If this happens, the amount of alcohol in their blood is so high that it is considered poisonous. A person with alcohol poisoning can vomit, become very confused and uncoordinated, have trouble breathing, and even lose consciousness or go into a coma. Alcohol poisoning can even kill you.

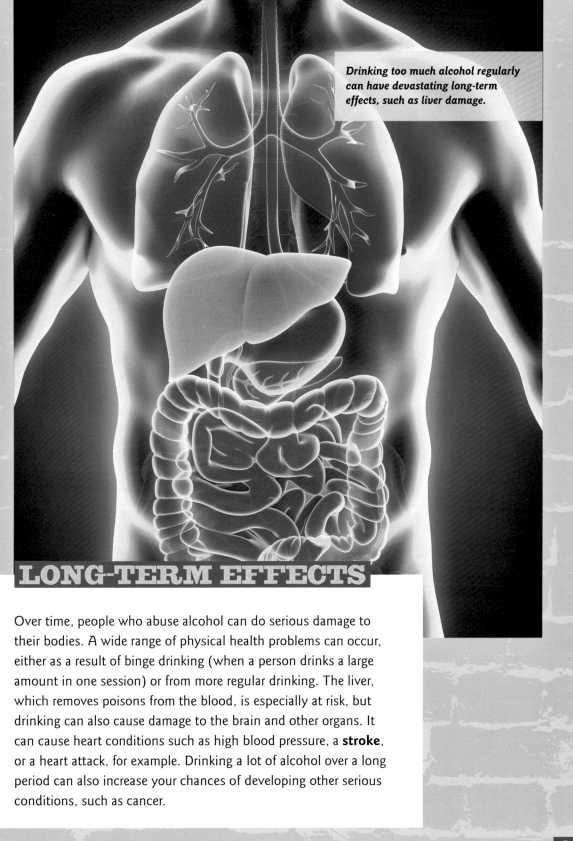

Drinking too much alcohol regularly can have devastating long-term effects, such as liver damage.

LONG-TERM EFFECTS

Over time, people who abuse alcohol can do serious damage to their bodies. A wide range of physical health problems can occur, either as a result of binge drinking (when a person drinks a large amount in one session) or from more regular drinking. The liver, which removes poisons from the blood, is especially at risk, but drinking can also cause damage to the brain and other organs. It can cause heart conditions such as high blood pressure, a **stroke**, or a heart attack, for example. Drinking a lot of alcohol over a long period can also increase your chances of developing other serious conditions, such as cancer.

Other Risks of Alcohol

Alcohol is a very dangerous drug, so do not be tempted to try it when you are young. As well as causing many health problems, it can lead to **alcoholism**, which is when a person becomes addicted to alcohol and cannot stop drinking it. Drinking alcohol when you are underage is illegal, and it can get you into serious trouble with the law, too. So do yourself a favor and do not try drinking alcohol until you are an adult. Then learn how to drink safely.

Alcohol can ruin lives. Do not take that risk.

WHAT IS ALCOHOLISM?

Although most adults can enjoy the occasional glass of wine or beer without experiencing any problems, some people become addicted. When someone is an alcoholic, they constantly crave alcohol. They lose control over their drinking and the amount they drink, and they cannot seem to do without it. Alcoholics find it so hard to give up drinking that even if their problem makes them lose their job, ruins their relationship with their partner or family, and damages their health, they may still carry on drinking. Alcoholism often gets worse over time, as the person develops more health problems. The risks of alcoholism are huge, and it is important to understand this because someone who starts drinking alcohol at a young age is more likely to develop alcoholism later.

Skills for Life

The risks associated with drinking alcohol are so great that many governments around the world have laws to prevent children and teenagers from buying or using alcohol. In the United States the legal drinking age is set at twenty-one. This is the age at which people are legally allowed to purchase or publicly consume alcoholic beverages. This law saves lives by reducing the number of people killed in automobile and other accidents and limiting the damaging health impacts. The law even reduces the risk of people dropping out of high school. The law is there for good reasons, so everyone would be wise to follow it!

Alcoholics can get help to deal with their addiction to alcohol.

Chapter 4
How Drugs Affect the Body

There are many kinds of drugs, which people use in different ways and that affect the body in different ways. All drugs have the potential to damage our health, because they change chemical processes in the body. Drugs can affect everyone's health and well-being, but when your body is still growing and going through the massive changes of **adolescence** that turn you into an adult, taking drugs is particularly risky. It can have serious and long-lasting consequences. While you are still growing, illegal drugs can damage the major organs of your body, including the brain and heart.

Taking drugs can affect your ability to learn.

HOW DRUGS AFFECT THE BRAIN

Our brains continue developing until we reach the age of about twenty-five. If someone takes drugs that upset this process, it can affect how the brain develops. The brain uses chemicals called **neurotransmitters** to pass messages from one part of the brain to another. To ensure messages travel on the right route through the brain, each neurotransmitter attaches to its own kind of **receptor**. This is similar to how a key fits into a lock. The chemicals in drugs can confuse the receptors and change the activity of the brain cells, making messages go the wrong way. This affects the way the brain uses and stores information, and so affects how you think, concentrate, learn, and remember things.

Drug use can affect major and important body organs such as the brain and the heart.

HOW DRUGS AFFECT THE HEART

The heart is another vital organ. It pumps blood around our body, carrying **oxygen** and **nutrients** to every cell in the body, allowing them to work. It also makes sure that waste from your body is carried away. Many drugs affect the heart. As well as lots of other effects on your brain and body, they can cause raised blood pressure, increased heart rate, and an irregular heartbeat. Some drugs slow your breathing, and can even stop your heart altogether.

Other Health Risks

Abusing drugs immediately impacts the body and causes other health risks that it is important to be aware of.

TAKING MORE RISKS

Using drugs interferes with a person's ability to think clearly and make good decisions. That is why people often do dangerous things, which could hurt them or other people, when they use drugs. Drugs can make people feel very confident, alert, and awake, or over-confident, arrogant, and aggressive. When they feel this way, they can end up taking very careless and unnecessary risks. There have been tragic cases of drugs making teenagers think they could fly, and so they leapt from a high place to their deaths. Drugs can make you more likely to do something you would not normally do, like have unsafe sex. Unsafe sex is when people have sex without using a condom. Unsafe sex, as its name suggests, is very risky. It can result in pregnancy, and in the passing on of sexual diseases such as HIV, the virus that causes **AIDS**.

People under the influence of drugs behave recklessly and often have accidents.

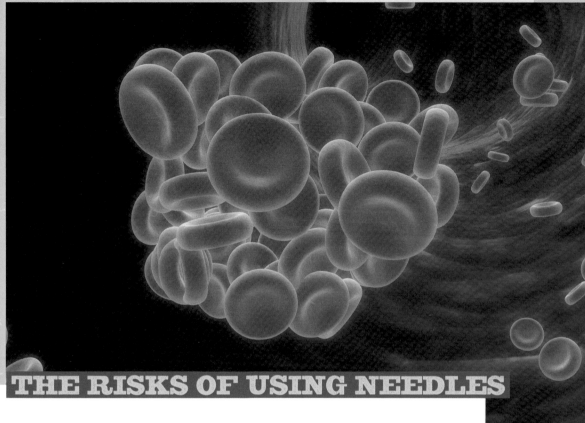

When drug users share needles or injecting equipment there is a real risk of passing on dangerous diseases and infections through the blood.

THE RISKS OF USING NEEDLES

Some types of drugs are injected into the body with a needle and syringe. For example, many people who are addicted to heroin inject the drug into their veins. They may inject the drug several times a day, and over time, the needle marks become permanent scars on their skin. Because people addicted to or under the influence of drugs are not thinking clearly, they often share each other's needles, either intentionally or by mistake. Sharing needles is very dangerous, because it can pass on infections with dangerous germs such as hepatitis B or C, or HIV. There is also the risk that the drug user's veins may be damaged, and that an **abscess** or blood **clot** may develop.

Addiction

Many drugs change the chemical processes in the body in such a way that the person taking them becomes addicted to them. They feel they have to take the drugs, and they suffer unpleasant withdrawal symptoms if they stop taking them. Heroin and cocaine are very addictive, even after trying them for just the first or second time. When you are young, there is an increased risk of becoming addicted to any drugs you try.

WHAT CAUSES ADDICTIONS?

Many illegal drugs are very addictive. After you start taking them you find it very hard to stop. People get a craving or urge to take more, and sometimes cannot think about anything else other than their next dose. Another reason for addictions is that when people stop using the drug, or are unable to get another dose, they develop withdrawal symptoms, like feelings of panic, sleeplessness, bad chills, sweats, muscle pain, stomach cramps, vomiting, and diarrhea. Withdrawal symptoms are so unpleasant that this can cause people to continue using a drug just to avoid them.

Addictive recreational drugs damage people's health indirectly by reducing the amount of money they have to buy food, and by placing users in dangerous situations.

26

HOW ADDICTION CONTROLS PEOPLE'S LIVES

People who are addicted to drugs find it hard to stop thinking about their next "fix" of a drug, or getting more of it, and this can easily ruin their life. Because people struggle to function properly when they are under the influence of drugs, they may lose their job. In order to pay for their next fix, they may sell their belongings. Some people even start to steal from friends, family, and others to get money to pay for their drugs. They can end up in serious trouble with the law. The best way to avoid becoming addicted to any drug is, of course, never to try it in the first place. If people do get sucked into dangerous behaviors like this, however, they can get help to stop their addiction.

Overdoses and Emergencies

An **overdose** happens when someone has taken too much of a drug, or combination of drugs, for their body to be able to cope with. All drugs can cause an overdose, including prescription medication prescribed by a doctor. This is another reason why it is so important to take the correct dosage of any medication you are prescribed.

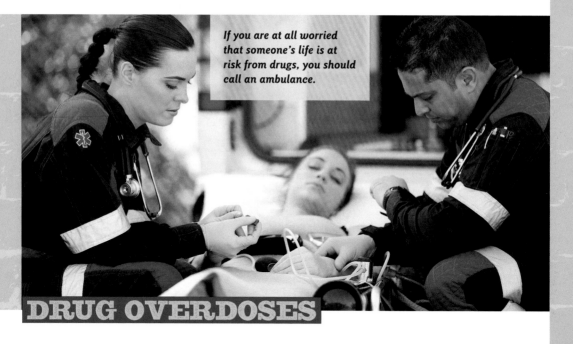

If you are at all worried that someone's life is at risk from drugs, you should call an ambulance.

DRUG OVERDOSES

The cause of a drug overdose is either by accidental overuse, or by intentional misuse. Young children may swallow drugs by accident if they find them within reach, because they tend to place everything they find into their mouth. That is why medicines come with warnings to keep them out of the reach of young children, who do not understand the risks of taking them. With illegal drugs, people may take too many and suffer an overdose by mistake, or on purpose. The body cannot deal with the poisonous effects of the drug fast enough to avoid the harmful side effects. Signs of an overdose might include unconsciousness, having a seizure or fit, experiencing severe headaches or chest pains, having breathing difficulties, and feeling extremely paranoid, agitated, or confused.

Skills for Life

You are highly unlikely to find yourself in an emergency situation related to alcohol or drugs, because most people do not drink too much or use drugs. However, just in case you see someone in trouble due to alcohol or drugs, who has hurt themselves or worse, this is what you should do.

- **Immediately call 911 for help. Even if the person is afraid they might get in trouble and asks you not to, you must get help. Their life could be in danger.**
- **Try to keep them calm and find out what they have taken.**
- **Try to roll them onto their side, so they can breathe properly and to reduce the risk that they choke on their own vomit.**
- **Stay with them until an ambulance arrives, and tell the crew what drug they have taken, so they can get the correct treatment immediately.**

If a victim is found in time they can be saved, but overdoses can kill.

Chapter 5
Why Do People Drink and Use Drugs?

People take drugs for a whole range of reasons. Many people take drugs out of curiosity, to see what they are like and how they make them feel. Some do it for fun, or because of **peer pressure**, because their friends are doing it and they feel pushed into doing it, too. Other people take drugs to escape from the problems or worries in their lives.

WHY DO PEOPLE TAKE RISKS?

While lots of younger people dislike smoking, and often try to persuade parents who smoke to stop, some teenagers who want to experiment with new things may try it. Or they smoke to try to show they are rebellious, or they think it will make them look cool. Many people have one or two tries, then decide they do not like it and never try it again. This often happens when people try cigarettes, because smoking is kind of unpleasant and does not taste good. It makes your clothes, hair, and breath smell bad. The problem with many drugs, including cigarettes, is that if you have just a few, smoking starts to become addictive and it becomes harder to give up.

Some people try drugs in social situations like music festivals without realizing how dangerous the substances can be.

TAKING DRUGS TO ESCAPE

Many people say they take drugs to escape from reality for a little while, or because they are depressed or worried about something. The problem is that taking drugs only makes things worse. True, taking a drug might make someone feel less sad or upset, or help them to forget their problems for a few hours, but the effect soon wears off. Using drugs usually causes more problems on top of the problems the person taking them had to begin with. They can become addicted, sick, waste their money on the drugs, lose their friends, and so on. It is hard to see how a temporary escape from reality is worth that high price to anybody.

Under Pressure

Some people end up trying a cigarette, taking a drink of alcohol, or even trying more dangerous drugs because of peer pressure. Peer pressure is when your friends or people your own age try to make you do something. Peer pressure can be a good thing. For example, your friends might persuade you to play a sport with them, or encourage you to get better grades in school. However, peer pressure can also be bad if people pressure you into doing something that is bad for you, or that you feel uncomfortable with.

HOW PEER PRESSURE WORKS

Some people say things to put others under pressure. For example, you could be at a party and you refuse a cigarette when a friend offers you one, and they say, "Come on. Don't be such a boring loser. Just try one." That's peer pressure. Sometimes peer pressure happens in more hidden ways. For example, it might seem like everyone is doing something, such as acting or dressing in a certain way, and you feel left out if you are not doing it, too. No one has said anything to you directly, but you can still feel pushed into doing or trying something because all your friends or classmates are doing it.

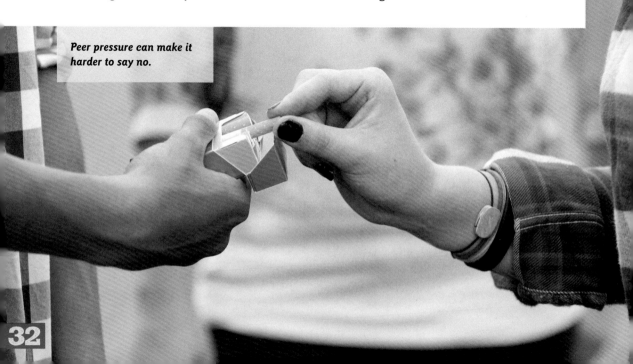

Peer pressure can make it harder to say no.

KNOW YOUR OWN MIND

The truth is that while it may seem as if many of your peers are trying smoking, alcohol, or other drugs, they are not. You are not unusual or weird for choosing not to. It is a sign of maturity and confidence to know your own mind, to know what is right and wrong, and to have the courage to stand by your convictions, especially in the face of pressure. It is good to learn to deal with peer pressure now, as you will face situations throughout your life when you may want or need to make a stand, and stick to your opinions or choices.

Dealing With Peer Pressure

Friends and peers may use all kinds of tactics to try to get you to try drugs or alcohol. They may put you down or try to make you feel left out or weird, they may try persuading you that there is no risk in just trying something. They may even threaten to stop being friends with you. There is no doubt that dealing with peer pressure can be tricky, but it can be done.

Saying "No" clearly is the bravest, coolest way to refuse alcohol or drugs.

JUST SAY NO

The simplest answer to give people who try to pressure you into trying alcohol or drugs is to say "No." Try to say it firmly. Try to sound definite and confident, even if you don't feel that way inside. You do not have to explain your decision. Sounding confident will make it less likely that people will argue with you, or spend more time trying to persuade you. Also, by saying no confidently you may actually be able to influence your friends in a positive way. Being confident about your position is sometimes all it takes to keep a whole group of people away from alcohol and drugs. Of course, just saying "No" will not always stop people from trying to tempt you, so it is good to rehearse some excuses and reasons for saying no, if you need them as backup.

Skills for Life

Why would you use that junk? It's really bad for you. I've read that people can get hurt from that.

I tried before and it made me sick. I don't like it.

WAYS TO SAY NO

I've got an important event tomorrow and I can't risk feeling out of it.

I don't do that. I need to stay fit. I'd be suspended from the team if I was caught.

No! I'm not an idiot. I think you just want me to get in trouble.

My parents have threatened to stop my allowance and ground me if I go home high or drunk.

There are lots of different ways to say No!

Chapter 6
Making Choices

We have to make all sorts of choices in our lives, but some are more important than others. Choosing to say no to risky and dangerous behaviors like drinking alcohol or taking drugs takes confidence, and a sense of **self-esteem**.

Building your self-esteem is as important as doing your homework!

THE ISSUE OF SELF-ESTEEM

People who are strong enough to make the best decisions for themselves are those with self-confidence, or self-esteem. They have a strong sense of their own worth or value. If people have low self-esteem they do not feel good about themselves. They may feel they are not good enough at school, or sports, or have fewer friends than other people, or they may be very critical about their appearance. People with low self-esteem may try alcohol and drugs because they want to escape reality or want to "fit in." They may feel like no one really cares about them, so what have they got to lose? Of course, everyone matters. People with low self-esteem may need help to overcome their feelings of failure and to start believing in themselves.

BUILDING SELF-ESTEEM

Some people develop self-esteem from a young age, helped by positive comments from family and friends. But you can also learn to build your self-esteem yourself, just like you can learn any other skill in life, from sewing to surfing! First, try to avoid thinking negatively about yourself. Turn negatives into positives. Instead of thinking, "Oh, I'm so useless at sports," think, "I really nailed that math homework today," or, "I'm so glad I took time to help my grandparents today, they really appreciated it." Try to stop comparing yourself with others, or thinking about ways they seem better. We are all different. Focus on your good points instead. Are you brave? Generous? Kind? Appreciate your positive qualities!

Try to make it a habit to think or say positive things about yourself every day, and focus on what's good about you and your life.

Pick Your Pals

Friends are really important in our lives, and they can have a big influence on what we choose to do, or how we choose to behave. We often make friends with people who live nearby, take the same classes we do, or play on our sports team. That's natural, and a great way to make friends. But we do not often consider how important it is to choose our friends carefully. Choosing the right kind of buddies can help you avoid the wrong kind of peer pressure, and make your life happier.

TRUE FRIENDS

True friends are people who like and respect you, and who would not want you to put yourself at risk of getting into trouble or harming yourself. True friends do not use threats of cutting off your relationship if you do not do something they want you to do. True friends do not make you feel small, or try to leave you out of something they think is cool, but that you know is not. If you have a friend who pressures you to drink or try drugs, they are not truly your friend. Talk to them about changing their ways. If they can't, or won't, then perhaps it is time to find some friends who do not use drugs, smoke cigarettes, or drink alcohol, because then there will be much less chance of you doing these things.

Real friends want the best for you and will not pressure you into dangerous behaviors.

SAFETY IN NUMBERS

In addition tomaking you happier, having the right kind of friends will also help to build your self-esteem. This makes it easier to say no, and these friends will be there to help you deal with tricky situations and peer pressure. If you have one or more friends who feel the same as you, and have the same values as you, and who are also ready to say no, this makes it easier for you to resist. It is good to have friends who you know will back you up when you really don't want to do something.

Take Care of Yourself

We only get one body, so it makes sense to look after it! Why risk damaging your lungs by smoking, or your heart and brain by taking drugs? If you make the effort to eat well and stay fit, you will feel so great that you won't want to take anything that could change that.

Healthy foods can be delicious and help you to feel good.

EAT WELL

During adolescence, your body is growing fast and needs fuel to get the energy and materials it needs to build longer bones and bigger muscles. To stay healthy and get the energy we need to live and grow, we need to eat a balanced diet. That means eating one or two servings of protein a day, several servings of dairy foods, and at least five portions of fruit and vegetables. We also need carbohydrates such as rice, bread, or potatoes at most meals, and should only eat small amounts of fatty or sugary foods. Drugs can affect the way your body is able to use the nutrients in food, which is another reason to avoid taking illegal substances.

BE HEALTHY

Everyone should try to be active every day, as exercise has so many benefits. Exercise is one of the most important ways of keeping your body healthy. Exercise makes all your muscles stronger, including the heart. This gives you more stamina, which means you can go on doing the things you love, like cycling or dancing, for longer. Exercise is also good for your mood. Exercise releases chemicals called endorphins that can help people feel happier and more relaxed. That could also be why most people find that exercise helps them to feel less stressed about things, and to sleep better.

Getting Help

What if you have started smoking, or have already tried drugs? It is never too early or too late to stop smoking, drinking, or using drugs. Either make the decision to stop yourself, or talk to someone you trust so you can get the help you need.

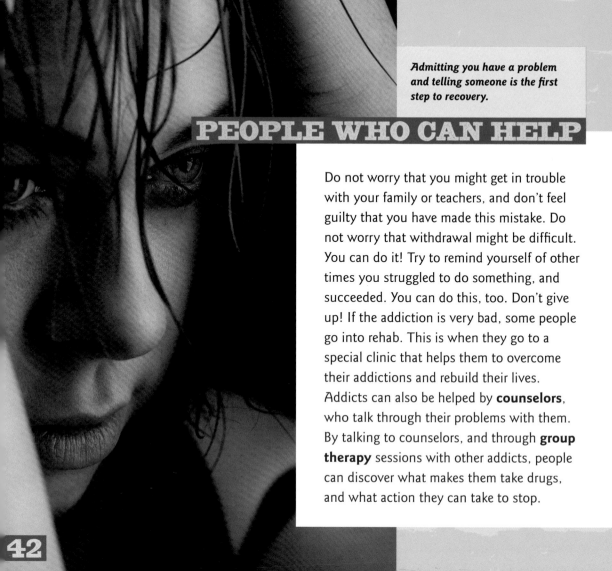

Admitting you have a problem and telling someone is the first step to recovery.

PEOPLE WHO CAN HELP

Do not worry that you might get in trouble with your family or teachers, and don't feel guilty that you have made this mistake. Do not worry that withdrawal might be difficult. You can do it! Try to remind yourself of other times you struggled to do something, and succeeded. You can do this, too. Don't give up! If the addiction is very bad, some people go into rehab. This is when they go to a special clinic that helps them to overcome their addictions and rebuild their lives. Addicts can also be helped by **counselors**, who talk through their problems with them. By talking to counselors, and through **group therapy** sessions with other addicts, people can discover what makes them take drugs, and what action they can take to stop.

It can really help to talk problems through with people who know how you feel.

Skills for Life

These are some of the steps people can take to stop a habit.

- Admit you have a problem and decide to make a change immediately.

- Think of ways to say, "No," and use them.

- Avoid situations where you might be tempted to take drugs.

- Ask for help from a trusted adult, friend, or family member.

- Find some support groups who can help you, online, by phone, or locally.

- Think about going to a program or treatment center for help, or seeing a counselor who can talk through your problems with you.

Happy and Healthy

Some people think about trying drugs or alcohol to see if it will help them deal with stress, or to make them look cool and interesting. They wonder if drugs will help them feel more confident, or have more fun at a party. Instead of putting yourself at risk, it's much smarter to find other ways to be happy and healthy.

The fact is that there are much better, healthier ways to feel good about yourself and improve your confidence than taking substances that can damage your body and your life.

MAKE THE MOST OF YOUR LIFE

If you feel like you want to hang out with friends more, join a team or a club. Organize movie nights or other events. If you need a challenge to make life more interesting, take up an activity like rock climbing, or surfing, or learn some other exciting skill. If you find it hard to relax, try reading a book or magazine, take a long bath, take up yoga, or bake some cakes. If you are stressed, make time to get outdoors and get some exercise, and sit down and figure out ways to reduce your stress. There are always alternative solutions to problems if you look for them.

It is perfectly safe to use drugs such as headache tablets, so long as you read the directions, but be safe and sensible and avoid illegal drugs.

BE SAFE, BE SENSIBLE

Life is all about finding a balance. Being aware of the potential dangers of drugs and alcohol does not mean worrying about them. Many adults enjoy a drink of alcohol without it doing them any harm at all. If you know someone who smokes, they can quickly get a lot of benefit from stopping. Just three months after quitting, their heart and lungs will work better, and after a year their risk of heart disease goes down. You, your friends, and your family will need to take medicines at some point, perhaps just an aspirin to cure a headache or perhaps something stronger. Remember that legal drugs are perfectly safe if taken in the right way.

Glossary

abscess An inflamed area filled with pus.

addictive Something that gives someone a strong and harmful need to have it regularly.

adolescence The time in a child's life when they go through puberty and become an adult.

AIDS The final stage of HIV infection, when a body can no longer fight life-threatening infections.

alcoholism When someone is addicted to alcohol.

antibiotic A medicine given to cure an illness that is caused by bacteria.

bacteria Tiny living things that can cause diseases.

blood pressure The pushing force of the blood pumping through the body's blood vessels.

cancer A disease in which abnormal cells spread in a body.

cells The basic building blocks of all living things.

chemical A distinct substance.

clot A solid mass of blood in a blood vessel.

coma Being unconscious and unable to communicate, often for long periods of time.

counselors People who are trained to give advice and help people with their problems.

crave Desire something powerfully.

dehydration When a body has less water than it needs to be healthy.

depressants Drugs that slow down brain activity.

diuretic A substance that makes people urinate more.

examined When a doctor has checked a patient's body to determine if anything is wrong with them.

fatal Causing death.

flammable Catches fire easily.

group therapy When patients with a similar problem meet to describe and discuss it together.

hallucinations Things that are seen, heard, or felt that are not real.

hangover A severe headache and other after-effects caused by drinking too much alcohol.

illegal Against the law.

inhalants Drugs that people inhale or breathe in.

inhales Breathes in.

inhibitions Feelings of shyness or worry that stop you from saying or doing something.

legal Within the law.

lungs The organs in the body responsible for breathing.

nerves The fibers that carry messages between the brain and the rest of the body.

neurotransmitters The chemical messengers that pass information throughout our brain and body.

nutrients The substances in food that we need to be healthy.

organs Important body parts such as the heart or liver.

overdose When someone has too much of a drug, or combination of drugs, for their body to be able to cope with it.

oxygen A gas in the air.

paranoid Falsely believing that people dislike you or are out to get you.

peer pressure When friends or people of your own age try to make you do something.

prescribe When a doctor authorizes you to take a medicine.

receptor A cell or group of cells that receives a stimulus.

resistant When bacteria resist a medicine so the medicine does not work.

self-control The ability to control oneself.

self-esteem Self-confidence, having a positive view of oneself.

side effects The effects from taking a drug that are extra to those it is intended to give.

stimulant A drug that speeds up brain activity.

stroke A serious, life-threatening medical condition that occurs when the blood supply to part of the brain is cut off.

Further Reading

BOOKS

Kenney, Karen. *The Hidden Story of Drugs*. New York: Rosen Classroom, 2014.

Paris, Stephanie. *Straight Talk: Drugs and Alcohol*. Huntington Beach, CA: Teacher Created Materials, 2012.

Paris, Stephanie. *Straight Talk: Smoking*. Huntington Beach, CA: Teacher Created Materials, 2012.

Waters, Rosa. *Alcohol and Tobacco*. New York: National Highlights Inc., 2014.

WEBSITES

Just Think Twice
www.justthinktwice.gov/drugs
Find out more about the range of harmful drugs that cause problems in people's lives.

KidsHealth
kidshealth.org/en/teens/drug-alcohol
Discover how smoking, drinking, and drugs affect people's lives and health.

The Cool Spot
www.thecoolspot.gov
Know about the harm caused by alcohol and how to resist peer pressure.

Be Tobacco Free
betobaccofree.hhs.gov/about-tobacco/facts-figures
Get the facts about smoking and its dangerous impacts.

Index